THE KING'S DAUGHTER

BY ANGELIA CROSS-COBB

The King's Daughter

© 2020 by Angelia Cross-Cobb

All rights reserved. No portion of this publication may be reproduced, stored in a retrieval system, or transmitted in any form or by any means—electronic, mechanical, photocopying, recording, scanning, or other—except for brief quotations in critical reviews or articles, without the prior written permission of the publisher.

Published in Hampton, VA, by Fruition Publishing Concierge Services. Fruition Publishing Concierge Services is a division of Alesha Brown, LLC.

Fruition Publishing Concierge Services can bring authors to your live event. For more information or to book an event, visit Fruition Publishing Concierge Services at

www.FruitionPublishing.com

ISBN: 978-1-954486-02-7 Paperback

ISBN: 978-1-954486-05-8 eBook

Library of Congress Control Number: 2021900978

Unless otherwise noted, all scriptures are from The Holy Bible, New International Version. (1984). Grand Rapids: Zondervan Publishing House.

A Special Message

To those of you who may read this book, please know we are not our own. Your life was already predestined.

I know you may say, *What do you mean?* I'm saying you were born on purpose.

Purpose: the reason for which something is done or created or for which something exists ("Purpose")[1].

---

[1] "Purpose." *Lexico.com*. Lexico, 2020. Web. 23 October 2020.

Table of Contents

A DAY IN THE LIFE OF A QUEEN	1
BE DECISIVE	23
PROTECTION	31
ORDER	47
BEING THE LIGHT	55
SOWING SEEDS	65
LEAVE A LEGACY	77
ME AGAINST THE WORLD	95

The servant who knows the master's will and does not get ready or does not do what the master wants will be beaten with many blows.

But the one who does not know and does things deserving punishment will be beaten with few blows. From everyone who has been given much, much will be demanded; and from the one who has been entrusted with much, much more will be asked.

Luke 12:47-48, NLT

Father,

I come to you just to say thank you.

- Thank you for waking me up this morning.

- Thank you for giving me another chance to subdue, to walk in your divine purpose for my life.

- Thank you for making every crooked place straight in my life.

- Thank you for moving every mountain out of my way.

- Thank you for bringing life to every situation I thought was dead.

You are worthy, Lord. You are my King, my strong tower, and the lifter of my head. My Peace, my Healer, my Way Maker. You get all the glory, Father. You deserve it.

Amen,

Your Daughter

A Day in the Life of a Queen

A Day in the Life of a Queen

Waking up every day is a gift.

The gift of life is indeed a blessing.

Were you able to wake up in the morning without hurt, harm, or danger?

That is a gift, a blessing.

Did you wake up in your right mind?

That is a gift.

Did you wake up able to breathe fresh air?

That is a gift.

Did you wake up able to walk?

That is a gift.

Did you wake up able to talk?

WOW, another gift!

There are so many things we have that are gifts from our Father. I know you have heard the saying *I wasn't born with a silver spoon in my mouth.* Many were, but the opposite is often true.

To those of you who are reading this and have said to yourself, *I know that's right*, I beg to differ. Maybe you don't have land, houses, cars, and a bank account with multiple figures in it, but you have *the Gift*.

I thank God for coming out of *The Valley Experience*. Being there taught me my purpose and gave me the push to continue on.

I remember telling you in the book how the valley was a cold place—a place of fear, a place where I was supposed to be conquered. But how can you conquer a person who is MORE than a conqueror? Not me, not *The King's Daughter*!

Leaving out of *The Valley Experience*, I left stronger and my spiritual eyes were yet opened. My Faith had increased and, most importantly, I left knowing who I was and who I belonged to.

The King's Daughter: yes, that's me!

> *"That which was sent to take me out had so much purpose. The King trusted me! When He knows you can be trusted,*

things that you didn't ask for will come."

Of course, we want all the good things, but when you can be trusted, expect the unbelievable to happen. Good or bad, ups, and downs. Tricks, plots, and attacks will come. Remember who you are and who trained you for battle.

You have the characteristics of a King. In the times we are living in now, everyone wants to be a King or Queen (or at least referred to by that title.) But imagine being on the radar every single day. Imagine waking up and wanting to just do nothing. Please imagine because being a King, Queen, or even The King's Daughter means you will never be able to do absolutely nothing. You are under the spotlight every day. In other words, you are a **target**.

"Kings are sought after and someone is always trying to take the Queen's place. The enemy is always looking for a small

crack of any size to slip in. Before you seek the title, be prepared for the attacks to come."

You must be able to stand firm in the face of adversity. Remain solid. Difficulties will come. Not every day will be a bed of roses as you imagined earlier. Coming from *The King's Daughter*, I had to take on the characteristics of my Father. When adversities came, I had to be centered. There was no room to be unsure of who I was.

I had to remain solid, unwavering. **You have already lost the battle if you are unstable.** Shake it off and move from your emotions that are taking control of you. After the hit, after the attack, after the heartbreak, and even after the test results are back, gird yourself up and look yourself in the mirror. Evaluate *you* even though *you* are the target. Look at yourself and see what changes need to be made in you!

Knowing the Word will help you to be centered. Remember, I John 4:4 (NIV):

You, dear children, are from God and have overcome them because the one who is in you is greater than the one who is in the world.

This very scripture will help you in some of the toughest times of your life. When you have the facts from the adversities, handle them as The King's Daughter—with great integrity, honesty, uprightness, and strong moral principles. Remember, the King lives with integrity.

You will be able to sleep and rest at night. Imagine doing something dirty to someone. Imagine breaking the law. Imagine robbing a bank. In other words, imagine having no peace or rest. The adversary won't have any rest but you will.

> *"The hits, attacks, heartbreak, and even the tests are all a part of the process. All of this is making you and building substance."*

We as people feel the more we have the better. That is not always the case! Yes, money answers all causes, but the more you have the more responsibilities come with it.

Look at the lives of some celebrities. We look at them and say they have it going on. What we don't see is how they have no peace of mind or the medication prescribed to make sleep possible. Don't forget about being preyed upon 24/7 with security around the clock. The flashy life comes with a big price tag that money can't even buy. Again, to whom much is given, much is required. I always heard the saying, *Be careful what you ask for.*

Looking at my life, I am a proud Mom of five wonderful children, a wife, and a caregiver to my mom who was, and still is, an absolute value to anyone she's encountered. Now her health is not the best. Things she could do, she no longer can. At the young age of 65, imagine having to depend totally on someone to basically think for you.

I ask myself why and how, Father, can I care for the woman who shaped me into the person I am today? Father, I have my husband who needs his wife's attention as you have ordained. I have my children who need attention and who have their ears and eyes wide open daily. Father, my children have so much they want to do on a day-to-day basis. I need your help, Lord. Show me how to do all you have called me to do.

Never in a million years would I have imagined seeing my mom in the state she's in. I consider myself a pretty strong soldier, but with this battle, I can't conquer in my own strength. Every day I put myself on the back burner—from the time my kids leave for school until they return home. I'm making sure my mom's taken care of from head to toe.

Mind you, the entire time I'm caring for her, I have to constantly repeat myself. Giving her simple instructions but yet having to have patience. This is truly a thorn in my flesh that feels like it's in my heart. Why? Because this is my mom. The one who gave to anyone without ever asking for anything back. The one who gave for over 40 plus years to her church family and close family members, cooking them meals. Where are they now? I'll tell you—living their best life.

Sickness hasn't hit them to the point that they are no longer the same person they use to be. I wouldn't dare wish sickness on anyone; I'm just saying that we all should treat others the way we want to be treated. Never forget a person when he or she is in a low place.

"You never know how you will end up before you return to the Father."

I remember my Dad, the Late Deacon Alfred M. Cross, telling my mom to stop. He would say, *Nessa, keep on doing for them N...s. They gon' show you one day.*

Did she listen? Absolutely not. She faithfully served her church family that she loved and treated as if they were her own family. Mom was the BEST cook you will ever meet. (I still have some of her dishes that I haven't mastered yet.)

The church family would pull on her for anything you could think of. If anyone died, you could expect a full course meal and more from my Mom. Trays of good, clean, delicious food cooked by the hands of my momma. Daddy would just look in disgust because he knew people's ways.

Mama was a servant with a heart of gold. I remember when she was an educator. She taught Headstart Early Education for many years. She wasn't just there to receive a paycheck; her heart was in it. She was passionate about her job.

If a parent couldn't afford to pay for a field trip, guess who paid for it. My momma. If a parent couldn't afford clothes for their child for back to school, my momma donated brand new items from some of the best places a person could shop at. She believed in showing love. She believed in seeing the good in any and every person.

As her primary caregiver, I have to pray daily. I have to ask God for wisdom, patience, and understanding. My phone stays busy but not from many concerned about Mom.

Friends who were with her when her bank account was running over with money are far away and always busy. It hurts me deeply but I find comfort in knowing when I help Mom with her baths (sometimes twice or more daily); when I dress her; when I cook for her; when I make sure she's dressed from head to toe, I'm sowing seeds.

Father, remember me, Lord. Strengthen me, Father, to carry out this hard but yet easy with GRACE assignment.

Thank you, Lord, for choosing me. I get tired, I get frustrated and, sometimes, I say, *I can't do this any longer*. Then I'm reminded by HIS word that says *it will never return void*.

Galatians 6:9 (KJV):

And let us not be weary in well doing: for in due season we shall reap, if we faint not.

So it brings joy to my heart when we're out and we see people connected to her and they say, *Vanessa, you look good girl.* Yes, I, The King's Daughter, did that. To whom much is given, much is required.

I thank God for my team. When I ask my partner, he steps right in. When I call on my children, and most of the time before I even call them, they are already on assignment, especially the older three. They are all too glad to help their Nana who loves them dearly and has played a major role in their lives.

When my mom was healthy and I was in school and working, I didn't have anything to worry about concerning my oldest three children. I often tell my younger two how Nana was indeed a jewel and the best cook in the 757. I remind them that Nana wasn't always the way she is now. They smile and say, *Really?*

Even in this journey, I take comfort in knowing my children are being taught the foundation of love and how love is indeed an action word. These are seeds that will bloom later and will produce a good harvest.

Just remember to love those who are precious in our Father's sight. Do all you can for those who God has entrusted you with. He will give you strength in the midst of it all.

Remember, God has trusted you in the fire. You will come out without any burns. You will come out stronger, wiser, and you will have

VICTORY. Your life will indeed be a testimony.

The King's Daughter. I didn't get to mention myself, did I? Nope, because being pulled in MANY directions, self will get placed on the back burner. People will take, take, take, and you will give, give, give until there is nothing left but for someone to care for you as I do for the greatest woman who is alive today.

When I walk out on the scene, I walk in Divine GRACE. No one will ever know what goes on behind the scenes. The King's Daughter must continue to walk in GRACE.

Days when your load is heavy—when you have no one to talk to, no one to cry with, not even a listening ear or one that won't run its mouth— remember, the Father, Your King is there. He yet shows me how to. He yet tells me NO, even when I think I deserve a Yes.

Don't puff up but yet trust and know it's all a part of a process. Be reminded "for many are called, but few are chosen (Matthew 22:14, NLT)." On days when it's hard, keep that TRUTH at heart. Remember, He has stamped His approval upon your life.

Every day when I care for EVERYONE else, I know I'm planting seeds (good seeds). Taking care of one of God's daughters is indeed a seed. She loves him. She cared for others when they talked about her. Wow, she's The King's Daughter too!

Have I given up on her healing? Absolutely not. I'm yet trusting the Father! Even in this, He gets the glory.

I'm reminded of Job who was indeed an upright man. He lost everything—his body and even his mind was affected. But yet he trusted, yet he believed. Even his spouse, who was supposed to be right beside him, doubted.

People will change up on you. The ones who you thought were solid will be quick to jump the fence and run. I'm here to encourage you and to remind you of who you are. We are here, sent from our Father to this earth, to do mighty things before returning to Him.

Do I get tired? Yes, but then I trust totally in my Father who said He would never leave me. Who said He would never forsake me. Who said He wouldn't withhold not one good thing from His daughter.

Every day I have to ask God for direction. I ask Him for wisdom and more GRACE to accomplish every assignment He has trusted me with.

REFLECTIVE MOMENT

I bet you had no idea that a King's Daughter lived such a hard life. Everything that glitters isn't gold.

What *Valley Experiences* has God brought you through?

_____

_____

_____

_____

How have these experiences shaped and molded you for royalty?

_____

_____

_____

_____

What small "cracks" exist in your life that are opportunities for the devil to slip in?

_____

_____

_____

_____

In your service for the King, what things have you put on the back burner that need to be addressed?

_____

_____

_____

_____

Who makes up your support team in God's army as you serve?

_____

_____

_____

_____

Are you unstable? Can God trust you?

_____

_____

_____

_____

Be Decisive

Decisive[2]:

- *Settling an issue; producing a definite result.*

- *(Of a person) having or showing the ability to make decisions quickly and effectively.*

As I said earlier, many want the glory but don't know what it takes to receive it. There's much one must go through to get to purpose.

Life, as we all know, is a bit of a challenge. Yes, life is beautiful and it is indeed a blessing.

---

[2] "Decisive." *Lexico.com*. Lexico, 2020. Web. 23 October 2020.

However, depending on our choices and the steps we take every day, life will be either what we planned or what we prayed against concerning our lives. We must be decisive at all times.

We should never be caught off guard when things arise. In other words, the warning signs were there. It is natural to ignore the signs and then have to go through the consequences of not listening or doing what we were supposed to do.

To be decisive, you cannot allow the noise of others to dictate what is the best decision for your life. Seek the will of your Father for your life. Everyone who says they want the best for you does not. Remember, as an heir of the King, you are entitled to gifts and I am not talking about tangible gifts. One of the gifts I'm talking about is called *discernment*.

Discernment is necessary. We are preyed upon daily as we enter various environments where everyone is trying to get close to us. Discernment is key and of high value.

Matthew 10:16 states (KJV):

Behold, I send you forth as sheep in the midst of wolves: be ye therefore wise as serpents, and harmless as doves.

In other words, **BE AWARE!**

Even if something is presented to you as perfect or it looks like it is straight from heaven, pray and seek an answer. Ask the Father for wisdom. Be decisive and prepare for the consequences.

Ask yourself this question: Is it worth it? You must have the eye of an eagle. Your eyes, spiritual eyes, must be extremely **powerful** like that of an eagle.

An eagle has one of the strongest eye sights in the animal kingdom and four to eight times stronger than that of the average human, according to some experts. If you study the eagle, you will notice that it flies alone. You will never see an eagle flying with a small bird. Take note: when you realize who you are, you won't be afraid to fly alone either.

The King's Daughter does not operate in fear but is confident in her ability to make sound decisions. Eagles are fearless. Like eagles, we stand bold, we conquer fear by faith, and we pursue the goal.

King's Daughter, be tenacious. Hold firm to what you got. Regardless of how high the eagle flies, it will never lose or drop its prey. This does not mean that flying at high altitude is easy.

The higher you fly, there will be a change in pressure. Hold firm and remain solid. The goal is to keep what you got—the promises of God.

The promises that are spoken over your life, hold onto them. Nurture them, work towards them, and speak life to them. Know that you were made for this! You may not have asked for it, but know that the Father trusts you with it.

Continue to be all that God has called you to be.

REFLECTIVE MOMENT

We all struggle to make decisions from time to time, but this level of royalty requires decisiveness.

In what areas of your life do you struggle to make decisions?

_____

_____

_____

_____

What are the distractions that you allow to dictate your decisions?

_____

_____

_____

_____

What is your level of discernment?

_____

_____

_____

_____

Protection

Protect your realm by all means necessary (Kingdom).

You would think after my coming out of *The Valley Experience* that all plots, tricks, and secret attacks would be over. Think again.

He, my Father, allowed me to conquer so I wouldn't fail the NEXT test. If you're like me, I can hear you saying:

> *No Lord, not another test, not another attack! Don't throw me or my children under the radar again. I'm in awe, disgust, and I'm tired, LORD.*

The whole time God is saying:

My GRACE is sufficient.

My strength covers you. I trust you.

You will not throw in the towel.

You will not make me ashamed.

My glory is in you.

You will stand.

You will overcome it.

You will make me proud.

I am reminded of 2 Corinthians 12:9 (NIV):

But he said to me, "My grace is sufficient to you, for my power is made perfect in weakness. Therefore, I will boast all the more gladly about my weaknesses, so that Christ's power may rest on me.

I get excited knowing HE trusts ME. Imagine giving your whole heart to someone and then it gets crushed or cut in half. Imagine trusting someone to know all your secrets and then get betrayed. Imagine knowing the facts, not assumptions, but yet smile after you've cried out. Imagine walking into your place of worship, which is the sanctuary, and having people look at you and say, *I wonder how she gon' act.* Yes, The King's Daughter was placed under a radar that seemed like hell.

Father, how am I going to do this?

Father, how can I walk right past her after she...?

Father, how can I forgive them after they...?

Father, my children have seen and have heard this. Father, how can I ever...?

Then to hear the Father say:

I have stamped my glory on your life. You will be an example to the people as I, your Father, am. I forgive them. You're my daughter and you can forgive them.

I'm here to heal you. I got your children covered. My angels are assigned to your entire household.

But we all know that, as amazing as that sounds, it is often not enough.

But Lord, I'm hurting. I don't want to see their faces.

Lord, people know. I have to see them at church. How can I worship knowing the facts? How can I worship knowing I didn't get an apology?

To which my Father replied:

The King's Daughter, this is making you the Queen I called you to be. You have been stamped with my glory.

Romans 12:19 (NIV):

Do not take revenge, my dear friends, but leave room for God's wrath, for it is written: It is mine to avenge; I will repay, says the LORD.

I had to be centered (solid), decisive—not listening to what people were saying in the flesh—walk in integrity and, yet, protect my realm (my children). I was speaking life to them even though their hearts were cut into pieces. My heart was crushed, but I couldn't fold. I had to be solid and speak life to myself and my children.

I had to wake up in the morning, pray, and meditate; encourage myself. I would look in the mirror and say:

You are more than enough.

You have purpose.

You are beautiful.

> *"I had to because my children were looking at me."*

They didn't know I was even pulling on their strength. The enemy thought I would act a fool, embarrass myself, embarrass my children, and embarrass everything I stood for. But, oh no, not this time! I will not return to a mental institution. I conquered that in my coming out of *The Valley Experience*, remember? I wouldn't walk outside of who the King had designed me to be!

I remember the first time I had to face what hurt me to the core at one of the youth conferences we attend every single year. I had a gut feeling I would see "Sis" there. Always go with your gut or, should I say, discernment.

> *"Remember, every 'sis' that you have ain't really your sis."*

Sis could be a wolf in sheep's clothing. *Sis* could be a serpent with a clever, cunning spirit, waiting and preying upon the perfect time when things aren't peaches and cream. When you and your significant other have an argument, she will have a listening ear only to use it against you later.

Be aware. A true sis or sister will:

✓ remain solid.

✓ tell you when you are right and wrong.

✓ never want what's yours. *OK*!

✓ pray for you when you are too weak to pray for yourself.

✓ help you to adjust your crown when you may want to take it off (most important).

A true "sis" knows it's heavy and that you just want to be normal. But a true sis will help you launch into your destiny and then clap for you when you get there!

When I arrived at the conference, I sat in my car praying. I had to.

> *Father, you have to help me. Father, I'm your daughter and I need you! Help me not to break; help me to control my anger.*

We are human. Even the Father has felt what I was feeling. But Ephesians 4:26 (KJV) tells us:

> *Be ye angry and sin not: let not the sun go down upon your wrath.*

I needed the Word of God to come alive in me at that very moment. The King's Daughter was facing a major test yet again. I was sitting there but I had to take the big step to step out.

After I finished praying, I had to encourage myself. *Girl, the GREATER one lives on the inside of you! You have nothing to be ashamed of. You are fearfully and wonderfully made. Walk as the Queen you are. You got this.*

As I had my pep talk with myself, I was wrapped in pain, defeat, and embarrassment. No one knew unless I told them. When I tell you, my Father had covered me, I mean He had me covered while glowing and shining. The anointing was covering me.

Daily I had to read Isaiah 61:3 and provide for those who grieve in Zion, to bestow on them a crown of beauty instead of ashes; the oil of joy instead of mourning; and a garment of praise instead of a spirit of despair. They will be called the oaks of righteousness—a planting of the LORD for the display of His splendor. In other words, the GLORY!!

His Word was alive in me. Every day I would meditate on that. I remember people telling me I was pretty, I was glowing. Some even asked if I was pregnant! I would say to myself *If you only knew*. But, of course, I would receive the compliment, smile, and say thank you.

During the conference, I remember walking right past the enemy. Oh, you didn't know? The enemy, the pure devil, will show up at the house of worship! I have no problem with you going to worship, but get it right. What's your assignment for showing up? I mean, really, what's on your agenda?

I smiled. I didn't make a scene. I didn't snatch out sis's weave. I didn't call her out of her name. Absolutely not. Not when I was shining with substance. To my seat, I went.

I went back to the real reason I went to the conference. Back to praising and worshipping my Father, the King of Kings and Lord of Lords. I thought to myself, *WOW, I passed the test*! *Wow, God, you did that!* Notice, I said God. I couldn't do that on my own strength. I was weak but HE was made strong. Wow, Lord, you are definitely building me up! Lord, this is all a part of the process.

I'm sure my leaders had already prayed for me that night. I left church that night a bit stronger. My character was yet recharged. Driving down the highway, I received a text saying, *I'm proud of you*. That meant the world to me coming from my leader.

I told you, we are under the radar 24/7. Even when we're asleep, the enemy will try to slip in. It's so important to pray before you even go to sleep.

Once returning home that night, I prayed before bed. I forgave the ones who had plotted against me. I had to release all the hurt so my Father would continue to release His favor upon my life.

This is necessary. Forgiveness isn't easy because the enemy will always remind you of the past. He doesn't want you to move forward. He doesn't want you to reach your full potential. He knows the greatness over your life and it's his job to keep you stuck. But I refused to stay in a low place. Not me, not The King's Daughter.

I want all that my Father has for me. So when the enemy comes to remind me of what has happened, when he whispers thoughts of doubt and unbelief, I tell him with authority to SHUT UP. I have purpose; I'm walking as The King's Daughter. I'm walking into my destiny and it's greater than before. So, I forgive so I can be forgiven. I forgive so I can heal. I forgive so that not one good thing will be withheld from me.

I trust God to perform His Word in my life. I know He will take care of every fine detail that concerns me. Thank you, LORD. He has a purpose and a plan for our lives. We will finish strong. Always remember to take what you have gone through and use it for your good.

Romans 8:28 (NIV) says:

And we know that in all things God works for the good of those who love him, who have been called according to his purpose.

It's only building YOU. Your character is being strengthened. Even during your healing process, you will have to turn deaf ears to those around you. People who are still trying to find their purpose are always the ones who love to give advice. They will say, *If I was you, I would've...* They will hit you with, *I'm glad that won't me.*

It never stops—the words from toxic people will never stop. *Leave him girl; put child support on him.* A word from the wise: stay away from toxic people unless you, with a sound mind, are the one giving Godly counsel.

I've heard it all to the point where someone had the nerve to say to me, *I'm glad I'm not you.* My response to them was, *You could never be me. The anointing cost.*

Taking direct hits from being on the front line can only be for a person who God can trust. Remember, even when attacks are launched, the enemy himself has to get permission from the Father first. Attacks come to the kingdom. The kingdom suffers violence and the violent take it by force.

REFLECTIVE MOMENT

Just the word "protection" triggers fear in the heart of some. The opposite is true.

Protection is a preventative measure, not just one when in defense mode. The Kingdom must always be on guard.

What areas have you left fully exposed in your life? What have the consequences for all-access, full exposure been?

_____

_____

_____

_____

What exists in your surroundings that you feel you need protection from?

_____

_____

_____

_____

What things have you felt the need to fight hard to protect that would be better left in the hands of God?

_____

_____

_____

_____

Order

A true King demands order. He practices order. He loves order. He breathes order. In other words, respect.

I Corinthians 14:33 (NKJV):

> *For God is not the author of confusion, but of peace.*

I'm a firm believer that peace and order must begin at home. Your home is your haven after facing the adversities of life on a day-to-day basis. At the end of the day, the goal is to make it back home to your safe haven.

I often say *practice what you preach, if not it becomes a speech*. In other words, you will be saying things and everyone around you will be saying things like:

Who is she talking to?

Bro, nobody is paying you any attention.

We are not perfect. All have sinned and fallen short.

But it comes a time in one's life where we have to stop and do a self-evaluation. If you aren't getting the respect you want, then ask yourself,

- Am I giving the respect that I demand?

- Am I living a life filled with order and respect or am I just living a reckless loose life and not caring about the feelings of others?

- Did you know how you live today could affect generations to come?

I Corinthians 13:11 (NKJV) is one of the most purpose-filled scriptures anyone could ever read.

> *When I was a child, I spoke as a child, I understood as a child, I thought as a child; but when I became a MAN, I put away childish things.*

Yes, in that order. When you know better, you do better, you live better, and you talk better.

I can respect a seven-year-old saying I made a mistake. But when I'm talking to someone and the person is 40 plus years old and they say it was a mistake, I agree to disagree. Certain things we just can't afford to happen. If you're 40 plus years old, you're on a level that should be seasoned with substance. You should be overflowing with wisdom and understanding, not making senseless mistakes that can not only hurt you but even damage your seeds.

As The King's Daughter, I daily strive to be more and more like my Father. I give honor where honor is due. I give respect so I can receive respect. I have a generation behind me that's listening, watching, and waiting for my next move. Therefore, before making any hasty decisions, I pray and I wait.

Charity, the giving, the love, the compassion, and the reasoning starts at home FIRST! Your kingdom is watching you. Before you step out into the world, before you step out into the community, make sure you are laying the foundation of a great harvest.

If I'm sowing seeds of discord and confusion, then what do you think will come up when it's time to expect a harvest? Let your light shine so that men will see your good works. You never know whose life you are impacting. I choose, it's my choice, to sow love, forgiveness, patience, and Godly counsel so that I may receive the GREAT order.

REFLECTIVE MOMENT

Law and Order is the plan of God. God is not a God of chaos and confusion.

In order to walk in authority, we must understand law and order and pattern it in our lives.

What areas in your life are in total chaos? Why?

_____

_____

_____

_____

What areas in your life do you feel are in perfect order? Who is responsible for the order?

_____

_____

_____

_____

What areas do you need to ask God to help you regain order in? List them and write your prayer to ask God for help.

_____

_____

_____

_____

Being the Light

There is a light that shines especially for you and me, so why not be the light you were created to be? A true King creates and inspires others to create.

Light is a natural agent that stimulates sight and makes things visible. It's amazing how the Father chose me to live so others could see His glory. Even through the hardships and struggles of life, His glory is yet revealed.

I know it's not easy when you're going through and things aren't adding up, but are piling up. I know it's not easy when you've just received a bad report from your Dr. I know it's not easy when it seems as if the enemy has launched a massive attack on your household. Take it from me, The King's Daughter, that's when you pull on the light within. You push, you pray, and you speak life. You boast in the hope of the glory of God.

Get excited in your sufferings. Yes, that's unheard of but **when you have a relationship with your Father**, you have to use FAITH and know that your sufferings are producing perseverance, character, and hope. You are the LIGHT!! Your Hope is not being put to shame but releasing the Glory in you.

Make a choice today to start first in your home. If you're married, be the "light" to your spouse. If you're single, be the light that you want to attract. And, my goodness, having children is indeed a blessing.

Think about it. You will one day be off the scene. What better way to live than to be the light to your heirs? In the other words, what legacy will you leave?

Day after day I give my Father praise for choosing me to be the best gift I could ever be to my children. A Mom is indeed a gift to the world. I've been out in the grocery store and I've heard people speak death to their own children. Hairs would stand up on my arm after hearing a Mom say to her child things like *You are stupid. You make me sick. I can't stand you.*

Then to hear them flat out curse at the innocent child. I'm like, *Help Father*! Don't you know your child is a product or a reflection of you? How dare you curse the seed that God has blessed you with? I can't say children aren't work because indeed some children require a bit more attention than others. No child is exactly the same, not even twins. Sometimes as a parent, you will have to take a moment to refocus, rethink, renew, and regain in order to be the positive light your child needs.

I believe that you must pour into your own first before you can take on outside assignments. From my oldest who is now twenty to my youngest who is now six, I pour in nuggets of wisdom that produce substance. Even on days when I just want to chill, relax, and have some fun, my six-year-old Destiny will say to me quick, *Mom that's not substance*! Wow, talk about accountability!

You can't be the light and live loose. You can't be the light and produce toxic poison. Light is the opposite of darkness. Keep that in mind when your flesh rises and you want to react. When nurturing and caring for your future, which is your children, keep that in mind. Ask yourself this:

What am I producing?

Am I creating a nuisance to society or am I creating a light that will shine when all echoes have broken out?

When darkness is around, speak life to your children. Raise them up to be leaders, not followers.

In Matthew 5:6 (KJV) it states:

Let your light so shine before men, that they may see your good works, and glorify your Father which is in heaven.

There's so much negativity going on day after day. There are days when I just turn off the TV to meditate and pray. I always give thanks first then ask for forgiveness. I dare not go throughout my day without first getting myself right.

How can I be the light to anyone when things are out of order? I believe children are some of the BEST investigators ever. You think they're not listening, but guess what? They are! You think they're not watching, but guess what? They are! Think about it: You have leaders on your hands; future Kings and Queens.

All five of my children always tell me *thank you*. It could be as small as a kid's meal from a fast food restaurant that they were so eager to have. They often tell me, *Mom, when I get older (or when I'm grown), I am going to help you, Momma.* Your children know all the sacrifices you make for them daily.

I'm trying to help you. We all come from all different walks of life. Some of us are struggling financially. Some may struggle with not having a strong support system. Whatever walk of life you have taken, whatever you have endured, can be a blessing to someone. Your children see the Superwoman or Superman in you.

I remember my Dad always working. He always provided for his family until the end. Little girls will always say when they are in the most precious stage of life, *Momma when I grow up, I want to be just like you.* The influence we have starts first in our offspring.

Your impact carries so much weight. We as people should get back to the place of influence. Get back to the place where the TV isn't teaching our children. Society has put a huge stamp on things like the music we listen to all the way to what we watch on TV. Some things are above our control, but what's so amazing is that you can control YOU. You can control what you do. You can control what you say.

Live to teach your children. Your light will be so powerful that everything the world is offering won't even matter to them. I often tell my daughter who is now fifteen, when you see me doing it then you can do it.

Your light sets the tone for standards. If your little one has always seen and heard cursing, drama, drinking, drugs, and overall a hostile environment, what do think he/she will become accustomed to? Yes, the Grace of God can come in and shower them, but when you have the choice to do better or be better, then make that choice and watch the fruit you produce.

A tree is known by the fruit it bears. An apple tree will always produce apples unless it's dysfunctional. Be the BEST version of yourself and your seed will produce SUBSTANCE.

REFLECTIVE MOMENT

Light and Darkness cannot occupy the same space. In order to walk in His light and be the light, you must create an environment that repels darkness.

Do you feel as if a dark cloud hangs over your life? If yes, how so? For how long?

_____

_____

_____

_____

Are there certain environments or people you feel a weight of heaviness or darkness when you enter their presence?

_____
_____
_____
_____

What things can you do to repel darkness from your life?

_____
_____
_____
_____

Sowing Seeds

A true King blesses the lives of others. I try my best to see through the eyes of my Father. I can remember years ago people were using the cliché, WWJD or *What Would Jesus Do?* What a powerful statement. If we would only apply that principle to this journey called life, we would see the change that we want to see.

Many of us operate in a spirit of selfishness. Selfish[3] −lacking consideration for others and chiefly concerned with our own personal profit or pleasure. How can one be Kingdom but yet only think *me, myself,* and *I*?

---

[3] "Selfish." *Lexico.com*. Lexico, 2020. Web. 23 October 2020.

We live in a world that is so full of greed, selfishness, hurt, pride, and much more, all of which are toxic and pollute the air. As I look back over my life, I can see the value that I have brought to the Kingdom. When you can see how a person's life has changed for the better, it makes all the difference in the world.

Our flesh will always want to please itself. Pride operates in the flesh just as selfishness does. I remember having a heated conversation with a close family member. The person stated I was selfish. Well, if you look at my life, even from someone on the outside looking in, you can clearly see that I'm far from selfish. You're talking about a wife, a mom of five, and also a caregiver to her mom who has Dementia. I am far from selfish.

I am a giver, a nurturer, a pusher, and vital to anything I put my hands to. All are part of the process. I sow good seeds to produce substance. I remember helping my husband plan a concert about five years ago. He was the special guest, *The Urban Prophet*. As he ministered to the people, I remember him saying, *I thank God for my wife.*

No one will ever know the magnitude of one's relationship–the growth, the deliverance, and the endurance that are vital to the Kingdom. Many have a problem with saying, *Hey, you saved my life. If it hadn't been for you, I would've been dead and gone, messed up on drugs.* Don't allow pride to get in the way of the blessing that God sent you.

Substance–sow the seed to produce it. Live the life that won't backfire on you. Your reward will be great. Your labor will not be in vain. You will have peace that surpasses all understanding. What better blessing can one have than to see that the way he or she lived helped others to become better?

Growing up, I can remember my grandparents planting seeds in the ground. Depending upon what season it was determined the crop they expected. It only took one simple seed to expect much more.

The seed didn't come up immediately. It took time to produce. The growth process is vital to the kingdom. The seasoned ones knew how to produce substance. They didn't just throw it in the ground and kick dirt on it. No way! They had to cultivate it; they had a strategic plan. They worked their harvest because they knew it was coming up. They walked in expectancy. I can even remember hearing them speak to the corn and say, *You're coming up good; looking mighty pretty.* In other words, they were speaking life to their seed.

I can imagine them saying, *I think we going to have a good harvest.* Carnal speaking will have you cursing your seed steps into the process. Faith will have you speaking FUTURE into your PRESENT situation. I've always heard the saying time heals all wounds. Timing is important in life regardless of what age you are. While you are planting your seed, you must first know the season you are in.

Remember to not become weary in well-doing for, in due season, you will reap a harvest if you faint not. Nurture and speak life to your seed. Yes, the Father knows you planted the seed, but activate the kingdom by speaking life to it. Refuse to release doubt and unbelief out of your mouth.

Realize the Father wants to bless you. A good Father takes joy in seeing you happy. Give thanks for the victories you have already won.

Having an attitude of gratitude will cause your harvest to overtake you.

Be prepared! Can you just imagine being overtaken by what you've sown? No matter what your current state is, think future. Expect the great. Often we put our minds inside of the box when we were created to invent the box without limits.

Imagine creating something without boundaries. It's called exceeding, abundantly, above all we can ask or even think, according to the power working within you. Sow your seeds on good ground and prepare for the abundance to return to you triple-fold.

You got this. You inherited the strength of your Father. Nothing is impossible to you if you only **believe**.

We as humans can get so frustrated in the season of waiting. The carnal side of us will speak at what's in front of us. We will lose every time when operating in the flesh. I dare you to tap into the "super" natural realm. There are so much strength and power beyond what you can actually see.

Most superheroes were ordinary people until they transformed into who was already there on the inside.

The change starts with declarations over yourself every day. When doubt and unbelief come, dismiss them by decreeing:

- I AM Kingdom!

- I AM somebody!

- I AM above and not beneath!

- I AM the lender and not the borrower!

- I AM the head and not the tail!

- I AM more than enough!

- I AM victorious!

- I AM a winner!

- I AM an overcomer!

If you say these things repeatedly and believe them, they will manifest! You will never be successful while on this journey called life if you don't know who you are.

Create your truth. Face yourself and fix whatever needs to be fixed, then walk in your own light today and every day.

You are divine. You inherited royalty. Allow no one to rob you of your joy. Some people are dream killers—if they catch a sniff of your dreams, they will work to tear them and you down. Never be that person.

Stand tall and take on any challenges that may come your way. Strive to be the best that you can be. Continue to rise up against adversity and keep your eyes on the prize. Stay focused.

REFLECTIVE MOMENT

Selfishness often seems like a natural by-product of modern society. Unless we are vigilant against it, we will find ourselves embodying selfishness. God forbid!

What areas in your life are you guilty of being selfish?

_____

_____

_____

_____

What is at the root of your selfishness? Fear of loss, abandonment, a lack of love, or something else?

_____

_____

_____

_____

What do you fear you would lose if you put others first?

_____

_____

_____

_____

Leave A Legacy

Jeremiah 29:11 (NIV) states:

For I know the plans I have for you, declares the Lord, plans to prosper you and not to harm you, plans to give you hope and a future.

Did you know the Father expected you to make an impact before you even existed on Earth? He spoke your future before you even came into manifestation. He expected you to leave your mark on earth. Ask yourself this:

Father, what do you have for me to do? Lord, what's my purpose here? You said you had plans to prosper me. How can I prosper, Father?

God is so awesome. He gave you a "gift" that could be used for His glory but also prosper you! Your God-given gift cannot remain hidden and must be activated.

In order to find your purpose and your gift, you must seek the Father. Meditate and pray. A lot of us are just sitting on our gift when God is saying, *I've given this to you, now use it*!

I am a firm believer that whenever something is constantly coming to mind, day in and day out, I believe that is your passion trying to emerge. Whether it's a book, a business you want to start, or a ministry you have been trying to birth, you will never be able to shake it because the Father has gifted you with it to bless the entire world. Live on purpose. Live to inspire. Live out your God-given dreams. Make an impact and leave your mark on this Earth.

A good leader leads by example but is always teaching others how to carry on the assignment. A good leader has a clear vision, is courageous, has integrity, honesty, and is humbled to be chosen.

As busy as life can get, there will be times when you must take a sabbatical to refresh yourself from the weight of others. Being a good leader, you will help people reach their goals but you also have to remember yours.

I take joy in seeing the accomplishments of others. People need to learn how to celebrate the blessings of others. We are some beautiful, intelligent, and powerful beings. Kill the jealous spirit or as some call it *the crab in the bucket* mentality. Learn to build up and not tear down.

We can all win if we would only support each other and learn from each other.

Adjust each other's crown when necessary. Imagine the impact we could make starting in our homes then spreading to the community.

Many of us have children. Children are expensive but they actually make us richer. Someday we will no longer be on the scene. After we have completed our God-given assignment, we will return to the Father. But, there is a but, our seed will continue to expand. Our mark will continue on. Therefore, we must deny any discord and confusion.

We crucify our flesh daily to produce Godly seeds. Our children are watching and listening. What legacy are we leaving behind? What will our children be able to learn from us to impact the world?

We have to think on a much larger scale than what we can see. Generation after generation will be affected, good or bad, by what you do. Many say you only have one life to live. I beg the differ. We have to live according to how we want our seed to grow and come up. Carnal thinking will have you wanting more and more. Carnal thinking will have you trying to do everything that feels good to your flesh.

Galatians 6:8 (NIV) says:

Whoever sows to please their flesh, from the flesh will reap destruction; whoever sows to please the spirit, from the spirit will reap eternal life. In other words, live your life as if your life depends on it. It does!

Teach from within and teach your light so that your legacy will live on. So many things have happened in my life. Not all were bad, although some were pretty painful and hurt me to my inner core. Yes, I wanted to retaliate. The flesh, my flesh, wanted them to feel the same pain I felt. I wanted them to experience the storm which I had weathered. I had to renew my mind and first ask for forgiveness for my own actions.

I couldn't allow my offspring to see me in a place of defeat. The enemy had a plot but, yet, I had to trust God's plan for my life. I couldn't risk losing all that I have worked so hard for. All of the standards I have set for my sake and my children would have gone down the drain. It's not worth it. Self-love is a priority and is of importance.

Take it from me, some will never see you for your worth. Those who know your worth will not only value you but respect you from the head to toe. Ask God for strength to allow Him to remove those who were sent to you to take from you. Follow these simple steps and you will be a better person:

1. **Learn from it.** Learn from anything that has happened in your life.

2. **Grow from it.** You can grow from anything, good or bad, and allow it to build up your character. Life's challenges will show you your strengths as well as your weaknesses.

3. **GO!** By all means necessary, if it's not helping you become a better person then you must ask for strength to be able to **Go** from it.

Anything toxic is poison and anything poison is deadly. Move away from it and build your legacy. His Grace is sufficient for you.

When there is a calling on your life, the enemy knows. He will use the very people who are supposed to be close to you to hurt you. The enemy never plays fair. He is wise, cunning, and very strategic in the games he plays. Be reminded of what's down on the inside of you and you will win every single time.

I've had people who have scandalized my home, name, and reputation. People who have turned their kids on me by releasing discord and creating an image of me that has never existed. I'm a proud mom of five beautiful children. Anyone who knows my true character will always be able to say I poured knowledge and gave above and beyond to anyone I could. Even now, at my age, I would love to have more children because I love them that much. And having the responsibility to raise up Godly seeds in today's world is a bit of a challenge, however, I would do it all over again.

Remember, I told you the enemy is crafty, cunning, and deceiving. So to have someone put toxic poison into the minds of innocent children is so degrading and just plain sad. Remember, these same children will soon be young adults. Who and what are you training them to be?

As adults, we can handle things differently from children. When leaving a legacy, we always have to keep that in mind with the way we raise our children. *Lil' Timmy* will not always be little, but he will remember how you acted, what you said, and how you responded to any situation. Then after years of him or *Lil' Susie* listening to you and watching you act like a pure fool, he or she will act the same way. You'll wonder why they have no respect for you, no respect for other adults, and no respect for themselves. All you have to do is trace your steps.

Remember when they were three, four, and five years old and all they heard you do was talk negatively about people who were simply living their lives? They heard you bash people who were not perfect but were trying to live the best they knew how and how the Father told them to live. You know, minding their own business and taking care of the many responsibilities they have while allowing their light to shine everywhere they go.

But you created chaos, discord, and confusion in your own child's minds and want peace now that they're almost 18. When the child or children have layers of hurt, discord, and lies sown about the very person who could've made a major impact on their lives, the end result is not good.

Take it from me, when situations arise, you have to allow God to handle it all. When people start confusion, make up lies, and use all forms of deceit against you, never stoop to their level as hard as it may be to not do so. Recognize what spirit is in operation. Identify it (jealousy) and pray. Leave it in hands of the Father to take care of it ALL.

A diamond is made under pressure. As a matter of fact, fire is also applied to produce the TRUE beauty that's hidden. Never dumb down to the level of their operation. They will use all types of words to get you off course. Words that you know aren't true. Keep glowing and growing beyond their place of misery. Remember, misery loves company.

When you're chosen, you will go through many tests and trials. You will sometimes feel you're in the fire and indeed you are. But the opposite is also true. Your feelings are simply an indication that something is happening or coming after.

While in the fire, remember how to respond. Remember you're close to something GREATER! Remember, under pressure and fire, the real you will be revealed whether good or bad. Of course, tests come to show us where we are and what we need to work on. Be of good cheer. Ask God to make you over again if you fail the test. Rejoice in knowing something POWERFUL is on the inside.

You are POWERFUL, VICTORIOUS, and a WINNER. Adjust your crown and show it to your enemy that, yes, you are more than a conqueror. You are shining with substance.

When the enemy uses a person against you, remember that is his plot to knock you off course. He wants you to forget who you are. But no, no, no, you're too close now! You have people assigned to you. You have people who need you to witness to them. As hard as it is when a dog is barking, you have to remain calm and not show one sign of fear.

The enemy, the dog, is only using what it can to intimidate you. Stand firm in faith that you walk in POWER and AUTHORITY and watch the enemy be scattered. He won't keep barking; eventually, he will shut up and behave.

Your legacy is watching how you will respond. Rise up.

REFLECTIVE MOMENT

Leaving a legacy centers or more than leaving an inheritance. Despite your economic position, you can always leave a legacy?

What is your God-given gift? What special reason did God create you for?

_____

_____

_____

_____

What thoughts or ideas keep running around in your mind or spirit that you can't seem to shake?

_____

_____

_____

_____

If you could snap your fingers and live the life of your dreams, how would your life be?

_____

_____

_____

_____

How would you have to change to live the life of your dreams instead of the life you're living now?

_____

_____

_____

_____

When was the last time you stopped and allowed your dreams to breathe?

_____

_____

_____

_____

How do your actions make a difference in the lives of those that interact with you?

_____

_____

_____

_____

How would you like the world to remember you after you are gone?

_____

_____

_____

_____

Me Against the World

Growing up as a child, I only had two sisters and no brothers. I was the baby of the family. In other words, I was the baby of the baby. So, of course, many called me spoiled.

We had a huge family on my mom's side. My grandparents had ten, yes I said ten, children. I have no clue how they made it.

I loved going to grandma's house every single day. I know we say *your mom is your best friend*, but I can truly say *Big Ma* was my best friend. I talked to her about everything. Whenever Mom would say no, *Big Ma* would say yes.

I saw her take care of her family and everyone else who stopped by. The definition of a true Queen. She wasn't conformed to what others thought. A true Queen is someone who's always looking out for the greater good of others. Indeed, she was a warrior, praying and protecting her family. Often, I find myself standing in the shoes of that great woman. I missed the mark by five in regards to the number of children she had, but I'm thankful for the five I have been blessed with.

So much has changed in regards to how we as a people care for each other. Not to mention the cost of living, the cost of food, and, most of all, the craziness we are seeing. Now that I'm older and can understand different principles, I can truly say those were the days…the good old days.

Even though times have changed, there are certain standards that I teach my family to never forget. For example, your home is your haven. (I always teach within first.) I love our family time because it allows me to drop jewels into my team/family. Jewels of substance and principles to live by daily.

My children vary from age 21 to six-years-old at the time of this book publication. What a big age difference! Regardless of the age difference, they will always look out for each other. When the time comes for any of us to leave and go to work or maybe just to the store, we never say bye but *see you later*.

As a Queen, I set the tone of our day. I give and show love so I can receive love. I let my children know that once you leave my presence, I can't think for you or answer for you. My daily prayer for my team is:

Father, continue to open their eyes so they won't ever be caught off guard. Father, sharpen their eyes, give them the eyes of the eagle.

Most of all, Father, sharpen their gift of discernment, Lord. Release an angelic host of angels to protect them, Father. Guide them safely home.

Each and every day He does just that. We are so happy when the end of the day comes and we can share our jewels—our conversations—together. Our conversations are more than that. Through our conversations, we are making memories that are more valuable than any amount of money. Memories last forever. Always create and value that precious time together.

The world can be a cold place. We have no control over the actions or intentions of others. We have control of ourselves. We have control of our actions. I often say to *treat others how you want to be treated.* It sounds so easy, but the fact of the matter is if someone doesn't know how to love themselves, how can you expect that person to give what he or she is not giving to him- or herself?

I said it's "ME against the world" so that I would never be caught off guard again. I'm far from perfect, but I use every fall, every hurt that I've experienced, for my good. A Queen will always remember this: what an enemy meant for bad, God meant it for good. Use those bad experiences to teach within first.

Bad experiences are only stepping stools. Step on those obstacles to build yourself up. Learn from those obstacles to move forward and never look back.

Step out into the world every day ready to conquer it, no matter what the day brings. Know that you are equipped to handle it. These are simple but powerful tools I use to teach my children. I remember my Mom saying back in those days that there were *certain things* you couldn't talk to your parents about. I never want to hear that testimony from any of my children. No, I rather them come to me and talk than have them learn from the world. The world won't always tell you the truth.

From the time this pandemic hit in March 2020 until now, we have learned what to put our trust in versus what not to. School was dismissed for the remainder of the school year. We had no other choice but to trust each other and hope for things to get better. Every day my children have questions. Even I have questions! This experience has taught us so much. One key lesson is PATIENCE!

Patience means you can accept or tolerate delay, trouble, or suffering without getting angry or upset. Wow, what a word! Many of us don't know what to expect. We, as a people, have so many plans, so many goals to accomplish, But, as we have seen, when the world/government decides to shut everything down all of a sudden, there's really nothing you can do.

You must always hope for the better. Have a relationship with God; that is a solid foundation. Anything solid won't fade or pass away. We must have FAITH in order to accomplish anything.

Why be so negative when things are already in an uproar? That won't help anything or anyone. Negativity is toxic. It will pollute your mind and even those around you.

When people come to me for advice, I'm slow to give it. I seek Godly answers, even down to my children. When they have questions and concerns, especially if I don't know the answer,

I pray and ask for the correct response to give them. During the pandemic, if I operated according to my feelings or my flesh, I would've been sick and possibly out of my mind.

Things are allowed to happen to catch our attention. Sometimes you have to turn off the TV, radio, and every other distraction. When you have purpose over your life, you must gravitate towards the things that are promised to you. Get silent to hear the instructions that God has for you.

Starting from March 2020 until now, we haven't lacked anything. As a matter of fact, we've been blessed.

- ✓ No one has been sick.
- ✓ My daughter, Jasmine, released her coloring book.

- ✓ Websites and businesses have been launched with so much more to come!

When you belong to the King, things that come to take you out will only turn in your favor. I can truly say that God is still blessing me in the midst of a pandemic. This time has brought about an even closer relationship with my family. He slowed us down for a reason.

I chose to build up my own temple first then I sowed into my family second, and lastly others. Priorities are needed in this season. Never get too busy doing nothing that you aren't producing **substance** and **values**.

Continue to sow on good grounds. Remember, the day you plant the seed isn't the day you eat the fruit. You must exercise patience and know which season you're in so you can sow wisely.

Never get caught up in the opinions of others. **They aren't you!** Be the person to break the cycle. Some cycles are from generations before you were born. Be different. Use failure for purpose! Generational curses are the WORST but they can be broken.

Many things may have hurt you, but do not develop bitterness. Allow your heart to heal so that you may have compassion for others who are in need of healing. You got this! Be stronger than you think you are. As a matter of fact, think supernaturally and, before you know it, you will see things manifesting for the good for you!

I am so thankful for my many experiences in life. Who wouldn't want to help others overcome the many obstacles along the journey we call *life*? Daily, I remind myself who I am and who I belong to. I didn't come to play games but I came to WIN!!

Knock me down and I'll show you how to get back up. Watch out; I'm coming back full force and I'm packing some real strength and DUNAMUS power. Tap in and overcome.

Remember, you are **MORE THAN...You are:**

- kingdom!
- somebody!
- above and not beneath!
- the lender and not the borrower!
- the head and not the tail!
- more than enough!
- victorious!
- a winner!
- an overcomer!

You are The King's Daughter!

REFLECTIVE MOMENT

There will always be periods of celebration and mourning in life. As children of God, we must learn how to count it all joy.

What things can you give God thanks for in the midst of your storm?

_____

_____

_____

_____

In what ways do you feel as if it's you against the world?

_____

_____

_____

_____

Do you still feel that way after reading this book?

_____

_____

_____

_____

Do you feel that you are prepared to live as The King's Daughter or are you still going through *The Valley Experience*?

_____

_____

_____

_____

How do you set the tone for each day? What tone do you set?

_____

_____

_____

_____

What things will you accept and no longer tolerate from this point forward?

_____

_____

_____

_____

What things do you hope and ask God for?

_____

_____

_____

_____

About the Author

Author Angelia Cross Cobb is a mom of five, wife, author, business owner, minister, and The King's Daughter. And that's the short list!

Angelia resides in Southampton County, Virginia. She married the love of her life, Warren Cobb, in the year of 2010. God has blessed them with five beautiful kids who support and push their Mom in whatever goals she set out to do. Jade, Diamond, Miles, Jasmine, and Destiny are truly Angelia's motivation. She believes in family first.

In November 2016, Angelia published her first book, *The Valley Experience*. The Valley Experience chronicles the dark places in her life and the battles she has won proving God's love and faithfulness.

Life can pull on you in many ways, but take anchor in knowing Christ will take you through. Angelia is passionate about helping others overcome any mountain in the way of a person's God-given purpose. Her life is devoted to God first, then her family, and then to inspiring and motivating others to know that you can be what you want to be. Angelia knows she may not be able to save the world but her heart's desire is to reach as many as she can.

Angelia Cross Cobb is a leader in her community where she led a unity march in the year 2010. In spite of the many obstacles that may come, Angelia quotes her favorite scripture, Roman 8:31 (NIV):

> *What shall we say in response to these things? If God is for us, who can be against us?*

Angelia has always been the one in her family that everyone goes to for help, advice, or just a good listening ear. She is the youngest of three beautiful girls. Angelia was raised and brought up in the church by her loving parents. They taught her that JESUS is the foundation and center of her joy.

Follow Author Angelia Cross Cobb at the **following sites:**

AngeliaCobb.com

Facebook: @AuthorAngeliaCobb

Her daughter, Author Jasmine Miracle Cobb:

JasmineMiracleCobb.com

Facebook: @JasmineMiracleCobb

Instagram: @JasmineMiracleCobb

The Family Business:

LevelUpArtJewelry.com

Facebook: @LevelUpArt2017

Instagram: levelupart_movement_

www.ingramcontent.com/pod-product-compliance
Lightning Source LLC
Chambersburg PA
CBHW021427070526
44577CB00001B/103